Fenella Gets Salmonella

and

other verse

Anne Smith

Published by Gibbons & Gibbons, Cricket Cottage,
Blackheath, Surrey GU4 8RB

Email: fenellasalmonella@gmail.com

Printed in the UK by Catford Print Centre,
3 Bellingham Road, London SE6 2PN

Copyright © Anne Smith 2012

ISBN 978-0-9574553-0-6

Anne Smith has been writing verse for many years, although much of it has been lost in transition. She is married with three grown-up children and lives in South East London. After graduating in English from St.Hugh's College, Oxford, she worked in educational research, teaching, advertising and as a magistrate.

CONTENTS

Alfresco	page 6
Bondage	6
Man in the pub	6
Comedian in the red fez	7
The last wake-up call	7
Coming up roses	8
Hippocratic oath	8
Left over	9
Composition	10
The snail	10
Idyll	10
Palindrome	11
Spy fishing	11
Lying still and roaring about	12
Heritage	13
Modern art I	14
Modern art II	14
Nouveau riche	14

The daughters of the intelligentsia	15
Tidying up	16
Grandma	16
Read the label	17
Proposition I	17
Proposition II	18
Flappers then and now	19
Cooper's ligaments	19
Specification for a dating ad	20-1
Mother's advice	22
The rat	22
Lothario	23
Death of a mistress	23
Bill, who lingered	24
Late	24
Libation	25
Maxim	25
Love song	26
With all my heart	27

Romeo and Juliet	27
Survey of a wasted life	28
Memento mori	29
Keep off the grass	30-1
Afterlife	32
Agnostic	32
Trust	33
Remembrance Sunday 1994	34
Undone 1994	34
Dons	35
Inheritance	36
First kitten	37
Last kitten	37
Invitation I	38
Invitation II	39
Funeral oration	40
In the next room	41

Alfresco

I picnicked under the wisteria
With Fenella
I got listeria
And she got salmonella.

Bondage

Dust and dirt are everywhere
Fifty shades of grey
I'm tied to the hoover
But not by a lover
And I simply can't get away.

Man in the pub

There must be some deeper
Meaning to life
Than all the worry
And all the strife,
'Cos if this is it –
What I've got the gist of -
It really makes me feel
Quite pissed off.

Comedian in the red fez

Tommy Cooper
In the funny hat
"Live from Her Majesty's"
And then he fell down flat.

People thought it was his turn
And it was, just that.
Funny? Not half,
Death always has the last laugh.

The last wake-up call

"What would you like to be called dear?"
I heard in my hospital bed,
But "When would you like to be called?"
Were the words that went round in my head.
Did they mean in the morning to wake up
Or was it the call that means death?
It gave me a terrible shake-up
And stifled my very last breath.

Coming up roses

Before too long I shall become
Manure to feed your roses
And that is when I can be sure
I'll get right up your noses.

Hippocratic oath

The doctor must do
One of two things
Either cure
Or help to endure
But never
Ever
Give the patient
Wings.

Left over

That last little bit
 Of cheese in the fridge, it
Really isn't worth bothering about
It's such a midget
You won't throw it out
Though you know you won't eat it.
So it grows a fur coat
And moulders day by day,
Until it runs out
With a backward glance
That seems to say
"Well, you may have kept me
But you never ate me
And now I've got away".

Composition

I am a cowboy
Capturing words
I have them in my noose
They lie still.

The snail

Beautiful snail
Like a small ship in sail
Upon a lake
Gliding across my path
Silent as a breath
Leaving the tell-tale trail
Of your silvery wake.

Idyll

Apple cheeks
Dapple cheeks
Leaves on a tree
Eat a ripe pippin
And think of me.

Palindrome (for Otis Ito born July 2012)

Otis Ito
Such a name
Born for glory
Born for fame
And when he comes into
His own one day
"O t'is Ito"
Folk will say.

Spy fishing

I grilled a fish the other day
It gave nothing away
Except its name and number
And to say "I was caught yesterday"
But I knew it was spinning me a line
Yesterday it was fine.

Lying still and roaring about

The dragon roars about
The crocodile lies still
Wrapped in his scaly coat
Waiting to take his fill.

The dragon blows out flame
But sly behind waiting eyes
The crocodile stares at the skies
And plays a waiting game.

The dragon can scorch and burn
He's noisy and full of fire
But the crocodile in his turn
Can wait and never tire.

The dragon's an amateur player
When it comes to making the kill
For the true professional slayer
Is the one who just lies still.

Heritage

At the museum shop
You can get quite nice things
Which take you back to the mystery
That history brings.
So why not stop
Spend a few pence
It makes sense
For in the far distant future
They may make facsimiles
And write learned homilies
About your trivia.

Modern art I (thinking of Peter Blake R.A.)

"Walk through the conceptual door"
I heard him plain as plain
But I have a perceptual flaw
And I bang on the door in vain.

Modern art II

To trap a fart
In a bottle
Is that art?
Then it's a doddle.

Nouveau riche

We want to show that we've come far
And have a bit of nous
And so we have some *objets d'art*
Scattered around the house.
Money is such a waste
Unless you have good taste.

The daughters of the intelligentsia

They used to build schools
For the daughters of the intelligentsia
They wore hats and gloves
And for their loves
Worshipped the lady games teacher
Or the preacher.

Now the daughters of the intelligentsia
Are down on their knees
And there are rumours
That in their efforts to please
They have thrown off
Not only the gloves and the hat
But the lawn chemise
(if it hasn't already been torn off)
And the serge bloomers
And that is not all.
The daughters of the intelligentsia
Have got their backs to the wall.

Tidying up

Shaving is now not just for tarts
You have to trim your private parts
And if you want to keep your man
Better not look like the Taliban.

Grandma

A dear grey head
Such gentle eyes
A loving smile
And words so wise.

Arthritic legs
A wrinkled fanny
Now who is this?
Your dear old granny.

Read the label

I boiled the soup
Impaired the flavour
Now I'm over-heated too,
Don't boil me
You'll spoil me
For anyone else but you.

Proposition I

I have a hunch
It's something I can handle
But though I'd like lunch
I don't want a scandal.
After the *consommé*
The consummation.

Proposition II

Who is Audrey
It sounds so tawdry
If he wants an Audrey
He doesn't want me.

I'm an Anne
Full of grace and *élan*
With a *soupçon* of bawdy,
That's me.

I don't want a chap
Who wants an Audrey on his lap
I just want a man
Who wants Anne.

Flappers then and now

Flappers had to bind the bust
It was a must
De rigeur
You had to be trussed
To achieve the required figure
For them the Maidenform bra
Was a step too far
But not for us.

I remember the time
Oh what fun
Quite sublime
When I was a 38D.
Now they've flattened
And flap
When I run
What's happened?
Slap slap
Ah me
Ah gravity.

Cooper's ligaments (look up your biology!)

Cooper's
Ligaments
Are figments
Of the imagination
To droopers.

Specification for a dating ad – last call

I don't want divorcés
Who bet on the horses
No sad alcoholics
Or mad workaholics
I don't want a smoker
Or one who plays poker
I'd like a meat eater
But not a wife beater
No babies or 'ex'
But upstanding at sex.
I don't want poor losers
No bi-sexual cruisers
No-one sweaty or smelly
With hanging beer belly
I want working parts
But I don't want cold hearts
Sense of humour a must
And one I can trust.
I'd like a Caucasian
I don't mind an Asian
Buddhist, Hindu, agnostic or Jew
Can all take their cue

I've friendship in view
But with the right fellow
Be he black, white or yellow
There'd be more to follow
Kisses in store
And maybe much more.
So where are you all?
If you are alone
Just pick up the phone
And give me a call
(and please don't delay
I'm getting older by the day).

Mother's advice

Don't do anything
Too impulsive
You may soon find
He becomes repulsive.
After the snog
The prince
Turns into a frog.

The Rat

I bet my bottom dollar he's a rat
He may be tall and dark and handsome
Yes, all that; but when he's got
Your heart to ransom
With his bedroom eyes
And moved into your flat
You may be in for a surprise
When you hear his snores
And see his whiskers and claws;
And that, I hope, will be that.

Lothario

Poor John, his legs
And knees have gone
Along with his libido,
Now instead of sex
He gets his kicks
From doing the sudoku.

Death of a mistress

Two old men
And a handful of ashes
So we see how passion passes
Mortal feelings
Frail as dust
Gone is all life's push and thrust.

Bill, who lingered

Why didn't he die
When he fell
In Sainte-Chapelle?
He cracked his head
Like an egg
But it wasn't enough
To snuff
Him out.
Come on death
One cry
One last breath
Then it's your shout.

Late

I'll never be ready
For death
I'll always want
One last breath.

Libation

We thought of the wretched sinner
Who'd gasped his final breath
So we asked his widow to dinner
And paid our dues to death.

Maxim

Hope springs eternal
In the human breast
And it never gives you
Any rest.

Love song

Two ghosts of love stood on the stair
I saw them though they were not there
They trembled in my memory
Those ghosts of love were you and me.

Blindly they hovered in despair
Within each other's arms they clung
Then sighed and drifted into air
Their love song gone unsung.

Dispersed into the night they fled
Forever banished with the dead
And there they seek each other still
And always will, and always will.

With all my heart

Do not think because I send you all my love
I have no more to give,
Each day love multiplies upon itself
And makes new passion live.

Those very words do breed love in my heart
And recreate new store
So though I send you all my love today
I yet shall send you more.

Romeo and Juliet

Shakespeare knew, for lovers,
What was best,
To kill them off
Not put them to the test.

Survey of a wasted life

He tried to fight the cancer
But the fatal question came
He couldn't find the answer
When they asked him for his name.

He knew the dice were loaded
When he heard what they had said
"No response" was how they coded
Him and gave him up for dead.

The boxes uncompleted
But another box quite full
The company depleted
"Here lies another fool".

Memento Mori

Not a soul walks down the lane
Not a soul comes through the gate
Only death lurks at the windowpane
And he is late.

The 'For Sale' notice stiffly stands
Proclaims an era passed,
The final contract changes hands
She's dead at last.

Removal men arrive in vans
Her worldly goods are sifted,
Only a fetid flannel hangs
To show that she existed.

Keep off the grass

"Keep off the grass"
No 'please'
Just a bald order –
Do it.
And so we meekly tread
The gravel path
And talk and laugh.
"Keep off the flower bed"
(Though you may admire
The larkspur
And the fritillary)
With the unspoken corollary
Not said
'Or you will rue it'.
Thus speak the powers that be
Backed by CCTV.
Until Jessica, almost three,
Stops as we pass
Points to the notices
And on her stubby legs
Steps on the grass,
Then seeing the flower border
Runs right through it.

A lesson in disobedience,
How we laugh
You and I,
But all the same
Feeling obscure shame
That she should dare defy
Authority,
Could play with it,
Get away with it,
And we cannot do it
Would not even try.

Afterlife

The Great Shoemaker
In the sky
Mends the holes
In our souls
After we die.
To walk with God
You have to be well-shod.

Agnostic

I'm battling against my God
But I don't know whether
I'm fighting an awkward Sod
Who never was
Or Who is, forever.

Trust

My life was fine
I trod the path
I drank good wine
And had a laugh.

I cheated sorrow
With a smile
Looked for tomorrow
Went the mile.

For You were there
To hold my hand,
To show me care
On shifting sand.

And if I tripped
On rock or boulder
You gently slipped
Me on your shoulder.

But when life's pain
Began to close in
I sought in vain,
Your arm was frozen.

I lost hope then,
You never stopped me,
And that was when
I knew You'd dropped me.

Remembrance Sunday 1994

Sir Peter de la Billière
Was there
Pushing a wheelchair
But not Sir Peter Harding
Who must have been in hiding
He could scarcely expect a pardon
For such a disgraceful hard-on.

Undone 1994

Caught in a sting
With Lady Buck
What a thing,
But what a f∗∗∗!

Dons (circa 1955)

Did you feel the burning yearning
To be steeped in God-like learning?
Did you feel a throbbing passion
That you thus the world might fashion?
Wisdom's store increased your ken
But you sought more knowledge then,
Ever seeking, searching, questing
Reading mind-provoking matter
Till with knowledge you grew fatter.

Now the robes of learning bind you
How inside them do we find you?
Unrestricted, free at last?
No, within them you're bound fast.
For the aim you sought to follow
Free of soul with flight of swallow
Shackled, tied with learning's chains
This the result of all your pains.

Intellectual conversation
Knowledge still seeks infiltration
Always you must question where,
Was it influenced by him
Or perhaps it was by her,
Tearing all things limb from limb.
Ah simplicity may well
Equate your learnedness with hell.

Inheritance

How strange to be called James
Like three daddies before you,
You'd think the paucity of names
Would really begin to bore you.
Is that why you call yourself Jim?
Well, you certainly could do worse.
At least you avoid the curse
Of being like him, and him and him.

First kitten

Our Kitty was a ball of fur
With needly claws and teeth
She used to clamber up the stair
And crawl right underneath
Whichever bed was handy,
Now who would be so bold
To take the risk of all those pricks
And pluck her out from there?

It wasn't me or Peter
It wasn't Matt or Jess
Oh no, it was our tiny Ben
Who handled Kitty best.
He'd reach his arms right under
And half his body too
Emerge triumphant
Not a scratch
With Kitty going mew.

Last kitten

Oh pussy cat
Whom I adored
Why did you go splat
In the road?

Invitation I

I'd like to be famous
Just like Kingsley Amis
So when I'm asked out
By importunate neighbours
And invited to dine
I can firmly decline
And talk of my labours
Of unfinished chapters
Of volumes to sign
And of critics in raptures
While I lie about
Drinking wine in pyjamas.

Invitation II

I snared a trophy guest
The other day
To come to dinner -
A writer
Witty and clever.

It always makes my parties
So much brighter
To say quite casually
To the rest
"And have you met Martin Amis?"
(Or whoever).

It's always a winner
Unless there's some ignoramus
Who asks "Why are they famous?"
Or says, even of such as Carol Vorderman
"I've never even heard of them".

Funeral oration

Uncle Eddy
Laid to rest
And the vicar said
He was one of the best.

His friends and relations
Were all so impressed
With the goodness of him
That they'd not even guessed.

His virtues were many
His vices were none
He didn't have any
No, not even one.

It's amazing how good
You become when you die
Earning your wings
Flying up to the sky.

But it's vain to complain
At what has been said,
It'll happen the same
To you when you're dead.

In the next room
(*after Canon Henry Scott Holland*)

I shall not be in the next room
Nor the one after
You will not hear my gentle voice
Nor my laughter,
I shall be in the hereafter.

I don't want to hide
In the next room,
It's not nice.
I want to reside
In the closed tomb
Cold as ice.

I shall not lurk around
Above ground
Listening and spying,
I shall be well and truly dead
After my dying.